4
Ingredients
kids

Kim
McCosker

4 Ingredients kids

4 Ingredients
PO Box 400
Caloundra QLD 4551

ABN: 17 435 679 521

FB: facebook.com/4ingredientspage
YT: 4 Ingredients Channel
W: 4ingredients.com.au
T: @4ingredients

4 Ingredients Kids

Photography:	Stuart Quinn Photography
Cover & Formatting:	Splitting Image
	www.splittingimage.com.au
Printing & Binding:	Leo Paper Group, Hong Kong.
	Printed in China
Australia Publisher:	Simon & Schuster
New Zealand Publisher:	Random House
UK Publisher:	Simon & Schuster
USA Publisher:	Atria Books (a division of Simon & Schuster, USA)
ISBN:	978-09-806-2948-4

Foreword

Last Christmas if I was in one bookstore or department store I was literally in HUNDREDS, with my beautiful Mother and team beside me; meeting, talking, sharing, listening and learning.

One recurring comment was that 4 Ingredients KIDS needed colour. *Soooo many kids learn visually*, through images, pictures, colours, light and shade. Then I realised, our children don't require a cookbook with hundreds of recipes,
they need the best recipes with images to inspire.

So my team and I started researching, we turned to social media to ask what recipes your kids love, what recipes you have in your regular repertoire, what was regularly requested, what did your kids make themselves?

The MOST POPULAR 80 recipes, the ones mentioned *over and over* again, are what comprise this Cookbook. Along with more than 200 beautiful, fun photos of our Facebook Family's Families.

Thank you to my amazing team and to you for your invaluable contribution to this cookbook.

Kids are 30% of our population, but 100% of our future.

It's up to us to arm them with the skills to nourish their bodies well.
Teaching our kids how to eat well, and how to cook isn't a chore - *it's our gift.*

With Love
Kim

Letter from a Parent

Hi!

I was just wondering what your plans are for the next book? (I assume there will be one?) Have you thought about targeting the kids market?

I have two boys very VERY interested in cooking, and I love your first two books (don't have the gluten free one) and I would love a book that was directed at kids, with the simplicity of your 4 ingredient recipes.

I know as an ex-teacher I would have used it in the classroom too. Just a thought ... I would love to know if you were interested in the idea ...

Thanks for your time.

Jenny

Table of Contents

Guide to Weights and Measures

To help a recipe turn out right, you need to measure right. I have included this simple conversion table to help, regardless of where you are in the world.

Grams – pounds & ounces

Grams (g)	Ounces (oz.)	Grams (g)	Ounces (oz.)
5g	¼ oz.	225g	9 oz.
10g	½ oz.	250g	10 oz.
25g	1 oz.	275g	11 oz.
50g	2 oz.	300g	12 oz.
75g	3 oz.	325g	13 oz.
100g	4 oz.	350g	14 oz.
125g	5 oz.	375g	15 oz.
150g	6 oz.	400g	1 pound (lb.)
175g	7 oz.	700g	1½ lb.
200g	8 oz.	900g	2 lb.

Spoons – millilitres (mls)

1 teaspoon	5 mls
1 dessertspoon	10 mls
1 tablespoon	15 mls

Cups – mls – fluid ounces – tbsp.

Cups	Mls	Fluid Ounces	Tbsp.
⅛ cup	30 ml	1 fl oz.	2
¼ cup	60 ml	2 fl oz.	4
⅓ cup	80 ml	2.5 fl oz.	5.5
½ cup	125 ml	4 fl oz.	8
⅔ cup	160 ml	5 fl oz.	10.5
¾ cup	190 ml	6 fl oz.	12
1 cup	250 ml	8 fl oz.	16

Oven Temperature Guide

Making friends with your oven really helps when cooking. Basically the Celsius temperature is about half the Fahrenheit temperature.

A lot of ovens these days offer the option to bake or fan bake (amongst others), as a rule, having the fan assisted option on will greatly increase the temperature in your oven and will shorten cooking times.

Our recipes have been compiled assuming a static conventional oven (non fan-forced) unless otherwise stated. If however your oven is fan-forced as a general rule of thumb, conventional cooking temperatures are reduced by 20°C (this may vary between models). So if the recipe reads 'bake for 1 hour at 200°C' that will be 1 hour at 180°C fan-forced.

Here's a guide:

	Slow	Slow	Mod	Mod	Mod hot	Mod hot	Hot	Hot	Very hot
Fahrenheit	275	300	325	350	375	400	425	450	475
Celsius	140	150	165	180	190	200	220	230	240
Gas Mark	1	2	3	4	5	6	7	8	9

4 Ingredients kids

Cooking Made Easy

Al dente: Often found in pasta recipes. It means to cook the pasta just until it's done, not soft or overcooked.

Au gratin: Refers to a baked dish, such as a casserole, topped with cheese or breadcrumbs, then browned on top, either in the oven or under a broiler.

Baste: Spooning or brushing food with a liquid — such as butter, broth, or the cooking liquid — to help the food stay moist during cooking.

Blanch: Placing food briefly in boiling water and then plunging into cold water to halt cooking. Blanching loosens the skins of fruits and vegetables to help peel them more easily.

Boil: The boiling process serves two purposes; it destroys organic impurities, and it transforms raw ingredients into cooked foods. Interestingly, boiling water is affected by altitude, the higher you climb the lower the boiling point. Water boils at sea level at 212°F or 100°C.

Braise: Slowly cooking browned foods in a small amount of liquid in a tightly covered pot.

Brown: To brown a meat means to cook until brown. You may brown the sides of a roast on the stovetop before cooking in a crockpot or oven.

Butterfly: Splitting meat, poultry, or fish in half horizontally without cutting all the way through. When spread open, the flat piece looks like a butterfly.

Caramelize: Melting and cooking sugar over low heat until it browns. "Caramelization" also refers to the browning that occurs during cooking.

Chiffonade: Thinly sliced strips or shreds of vegetables or herbs.

Cream: Rapidly mixing one or more ingredients with a spoon or mixer until smooth and creamy. When you cream butter or other fats, the mixture also becomes fluffy because air is incorporated during the rapid mixing process.

Curdle: Separation of a mixture into a liquid with solid particles. For example, soured milk curdles.

Deglaze: Adding a liquid to a pan in which food has been browned, and heating it to loosen the cooked food particles.

Dice: This liquid is usually thickened to make a flavourful sauce.

Dice: To dice is like to chop, but the pieces are smaller.

Dredge: Coating a food lightly with flour, breadcrumbs, or cornmeal.

French: Cutting a meat or vegetable lengthwise into very thin strips.

Grate: To reduce to fragments, shreds, or powder by rubbing against an abrasive surface often a kitchen tool called a 'grater.'

Julienne: To cut a fruit or vegetable into matchstick strips about 2 inches long.

Marinate: To take food and soak it in a mixture of spices, oil, and possibly vinegar to make it more tender and flavourful. You can generally marinate food for half an hour to days depending on the dish.

Mince: Cutting food into very fine pieces.

Reduce: Boiling a liquid in an uncovered pot or pan to evaporate some of the liquid. This reduces the volume, concentrates the flavour, and thickens the mixture.

Sauté: Cooking and stirring a food in a small amount of fat over direct heat.

Score: To make shallow cuts in the surface of a food just before cooking or baking.

Sear: Using high heat to quickly brown the surface of a food to seal in the juices. Foods can be seared in a very hot pan or under the broiler.

Slicing: Is when you cut completely through an object. Think of slicing cheese, or bread. Same principle goes for veggies, meat and fruit.

Simmer: Slowly cooking food in a liquid just below the boiling point. Tiny bubbles may break the surface.

Steam: Steaming is the cooking of foods by steam (moist heat) under varying degrees of pressure.

Steep: Soaking dry ingredients in a hot liquid to infuse it with flavour and colour, as with tea or coffee.

Sweat: Cooking food over low heat in a small amount of fat in a covered pot or pan so it cooks in its own juices until soft but not browned.

Zest: The peel or coloured part of citrus fruit skin, which contains flavourful oils. (The white pith is not part of the zest, and has a bitter taste.)

Kitchen Safety & Hygiene Tips for Kids

Cooking is a life skill and provides kids with a hands-on experience that teaches a valuable lifelong skill. Engaging kids in the kitchen at an early age builds a strong foundation for successful cooking practices. Safety is a big part of cooking. Set the ground rules before your child picks up his first whisk or spatula. The kitchen is full of potential dangers, making it essential to teach your child how to behave in the area.

Clean Hands

The first line of defence against germs is to WASH YOUR HANDS! Good hand washing will resist against the spread of many illnesses, from the common cold to more serious illnesses such as meningitis, bronchiolitis, influenza, Hepatitis A, and most types of infectious diarrhea.

Supervision

With knives, appliances and heat sources in the kitchen, adult supervision is a must for any cooking activity with kids. An adult can help assess the potential dangers and keep the kids from them. An adult in the kitchen also ensures the kids will use the kitchen equipment properly and practice the other kitchen safety rules.

Restricted Activities

The ages of the kids involved influences what kitchen activities they can handle. Assess your child's age and maturity level to determine which kitchen duties should be restricted for them. Younger kids shouldn't handle sharp knives because of the risk of cuts, but they might be able to handle a dull butter knife if it will do. If a sharp knife is necessary, an adult should handle the cutting. The use of the stove and oven should be reserved for older kids.

Proper Utensil Usage

Kids need to practice using all kitchen utensils and appliances properly. Demonstrate how to use utensils, such as spatulas, whisks and egg beaters. Think about the types of utensils you use on a regular basis in the kitchen and include them in the demonstration. Do the same with small appliances, such as mixers, blenders and toasters. Using these tools might seem like common knowledge, but kids might not know all of the proper uses and safety rules for them.

Food Handling

Kids also need guidance on proper food handling. If they are helping with meals that involve meat, instruct them on the importance of washing your hands and the work area after preparing the meat. Emphasise that no other foods should go on the surfaces until they are clean. Storing cold foods in the refrigerator is another important lesson for the kids. Teach them to put leftovers in the refrigerator right away so harmful bacteria doesn't form.

Cleaning

Cleaning the kitchen properly is a matter of safety that kids should address. Leaving remnants of food can lead to contamination of other food items. Show kids how to clean the surfaces and remind them to clean immediately after finishing the task. Discuss where different waste materials go. If you have a compost bin, teach them which items go in it. If you recycle, talk to the kids about the packaging and items that can be reused or recycled.

Plastic Utensils

Plastic spatulas, measuring cups, bowls and dishes are light-weight in the hands of little helpers.

Kitchen Best-Practices

- *Always turn handles inward when cooking on the stovetop — away from prying fingers*
- *Never place hot food or drinks on a surface that kids can reach*
- *Always have an adult present for the 'unexpecteds!'*
- *Keep it simple and have fun!*

Healthy Habits

To help you choose foods with the right mix of essential nutrients for your growing kids, the Australian Healthy Eating Guidelines recommend basing your diet on the Five Food Groups. To stay healthy, it's recommended you eat a certain number of serves from each of these five groups every day.

FOOD GROUP	DAILY SERVES
Vegetables	5
Breads, cereals, rice, pasta and noodles	5–9
Fruit	2
Milk, yoghurt and cheese	2–4
Meat, fish, poultry, eggs, nuts and legumes	1–2

It seems appropriate to introduce you to a dear friend and colleague, Mr. Veggie-Smuggler (Mr. VS). He will appear regularly throughout this book, with ideas on how to incorporate more veggies into everyday meals.

An Active Life

Childhood obesity is one of the most serious public health challenges of the 21st century. You've probably all heard the statistics from around the world; a quick 'Google' search tells you that 1 in 4 children in Australia and the UK are overweight, 1 in 3 in the USA and rates growing at an alarming pace.

While many factors contribute to this, here are some practical suggestions we have learnt to help fight obesity from a variety of both health experts and active families.

1. **Play:** Encourage your kids and grandkids to get at least 60 minutes of daily physical activity every single day.

2. **Let your children have their say:** Get them involved in your weekly menus, the more input and interest they display, the more likelihood you have of getting them to eat their meals (or hopefully at least to try them).

3. **Unplug at meal times:** We know it's so very hard to turn off the TV, and leave the iPhone or iPad in the office at mealtimes … But we have to TRY! Try to have at least one sit-down meal every day together as a family, use this as your time for conversation and connection.

4. **Keep it on hand:** Keep a supply of nutritious snack foods like fruit, veggies, nuts, legumes, whole-grain crackers, breads and cereals on hand. Cut them into bite-sized pieces to make them more inviting, a child is more likely to grab a piece of watermelon than a watermelon.

5. **Be a good role model:** 'Monkey see; Monkey do.' Set a good example by serving reasonable portions, eating lots of fresh fruits and veggies, drinking lots of water and exercising daily (mental note; must walk more regularly!)

6. **Eat Breakfast:** Of all the meals do not skip brekky as it is the most important meal of the day. Not only is brekky linked to better brain function in kids, it also jump starts the metabolism.

7. **Cut down on:** TV, computer and video games and sitting for more than 30 minutes at a time.

8. **3–5 times a week try and fit in some 'aerobic' activity:** Jogging, rollerblading, skateboarding, volleyball, netball, soccer, rugby or whatever activity that gets your heart rate 'up.'

9. **2–3 times a week engage in 'leisure' activities:** Tennis, canoeing, bike riding, fishing, surfing, swimming or whatever activity gets you up and active.

What's 4 BreKky?

A Breakfast Box

Serves 2

- ¾ cup (185g) vanilla yoghurt
- 1 small banana, sliced
- 8 strawberries, hulled and quartered
- ½ cup (55g) granola, plus extra for topping

Layer the ingredients into a parfait glass or pretty box beginning with the fruit, then yoghurt, and then cereal. Repeat two more times to finish with a layer of cereal on top. Garnish with a strawberry or berry of choice.

Serve it with a nutritious shake like our Banana-Bix Shake: 1 banana, 1½ cups (375ml) milk, 1 Weet-Bix (or 2 to 3 tablespoons of your kids' favourite whole-grain cereal) and 1 teaspoon of honey, blend all ingredients together until nice and smooth.

Berry Blast

[f] *Submitted by Chellie Mantell.*

Serves 1

- *½ cup (55g) berry muesli*
- *½ cup (125ml) apple juice*
- *½ green or Pink Lady apple, grated*
- *2 tablespoons yoghurt*

Place the muesli and apple juice in a bowl and stir to combine. Cover with cling film and soak overnight. In the morning, stir in the grated apple and yoghurt.

Optional: Garnish with blueberries 'brain berries', or any seasonal fruit.

Brekky Bars

Makes 12

- *1½ cups (150g) quick oatmeal*
- *¼ cup (45g) whole-wheat flour*
- *¼ cup (60ml) orange juice*
- *1½ cups grated apple*

Preheat oven 180°C. Place all the ingredients together in a bowl. Wet your hands and begin to mix. Mixing this way will help extract additional juice from the apples. When combined, press the mixture into a paper-lined 8 x 20cm bar tray, smooth over the top with the base of a tablespoon. Bake for 25 to 30 minutes or until golden in colour. Remove from the baking dish and cut while still warm.

Optional: Add half a cup of sultanas or chopped dates and sprinkle with cinnamon and nutmeg.

Flat Hash Browns

Makes 12

- *4 potatoes, peeled*
- *1¼ cups grated cheddar cheese*
- *¼ cup (60ml) vegetable oil, to shallow fry*

Coarsely grate the potatoes, then use your hands to squeeze out as much excess liquid as possible and transfer to a bowl. Stir in the Cheddar and season to taste. In a large nonstick frying pan, heat two tablespoons of the oil until shimmering, not smoking. Place four quarter-cup portions of the potato mixture in the pan and flatten each with a spatula. Cook over medium heat for 2 minutes or until browned on one side. Using an egg flip, turn and cook the other side. Transfer the hash browns to a baking tray lined with paper towel and place in a moderate oven to keep warm. Repeat in two more batches with the remaining mixture, reheating and topping up oil between batches if necessary.

 Grate in a little onion, carrot or zucchini, finely chop some capsicum (pepper) or sweet potato, all are healthy additions to the humble hash brown!

Green Eggs & Ham

Serves 1

- *1 egg, whisked*
- *1 teaspoon chopped, fresh chives*
- *2 slices honey ham, thinly sliced*
- *1 slice whole grain toast*

Heat a 20cm nonstick frying pan to low heat. In a small bowl, whisk the egg and 2 tablespoons of water until light and fluffy. Slice the ham thinly and set aside with the chives. Push your toast down now as the eggs cook very quickly! Pour the egg into the saucepan and stir constantly for about 1 minute, or until it becomes slightly firm. Stir through the ham and chives and serve with toast. Your egg is ready when there are no runny bits!

 Plant a herb in a small pot with your child. Parsley is the world's most popular herb and is a giant in terms of health benefits. Chives and mint are great herbs to plant as they are very hard to kill!

Purple Pancakes

Recipe by Jodie Mannion.

Makes 10 ❄

- *1 cup (175g) self-raising whole wheat flour*
- *1 cup (250ml) milk*
- *1 egg, beaten*
- *½ cup mixed berries*

In a bowl, lightly whisk together the flour, milk, and egg until all lumps are gone. Gently stir in the berries. Heat a nonstick frying pan over medium heat. Using a quarter cup measure, dollop three lots of mixture into the pan. Once they begin to bubble evenly, flip and cook the other side until the bottom is lightly golden. Repeat until all the batter is gone.

Optional: Serve topped with yoghurt and frozen or fresh berries.

You**Tube** *4 Ingredients Channel / Choc-Chip Pancakes*

Volcanic Eggs

Cheryl Jensen wrote, "This takes a little while, but it's worth it!"

Makes 4

- *4 eggs, separated*
- *4 slices wholemeal bread, crusts removed*
- *1 cup grated Parmesan cheese*

Preheat the oven to 180°C. In a bowl, with an electric beater, beat the egg whites until stiff peaks form. Line a baking tray with baking paper. Place the bread on the baking tray. Spoon a mound of egg white onto each slice, then make a little crevice on the very top and gently place the egg yolk in it. Sprinkle with Parmesan and a grind of black pepper (the volcanic ash). Bake until the egg white is firm, the cheese melted, and the egg yolk runny when you cut into it (molten lava), 8 to 12 minutes.

Artist: Hamilton Turnbull

Snack Attack

Apricot Baskets

Serves 4

- *4 fresh apricots, halved and pitted*
- *¼ cup cottage cheese*
- *1 teaspoon cinnamon*
- *2 tablespoons honey*

Fill each apricot half with cottage cheese. Add a sprinkle of cinnamon and drizzle with the honey.

Tip: Apricots are low in sodium, calories and fat. They are high in vitamins A and C and are a good source of potassium. The fruit also contains phosphorus, iron, fibre and calcium. Choose fresh apricots that are well-formed, plump and fairly firm. Refrigerate ripe apricots and if too firm, ripen at room temperature in a brown paper bag with a banana or an apple.

Caramel Cookies

Add the word 'caramel' to anything and instantly its appeal increases.

Makes 20

- *½ cup (115g) butter, at room temperature*
- *½ cup (110g) packed brown sugar*
- *2 tablespoons golden syrup*
- *1 cup (175g) self-raising flour*

Preheat oven 180°C. In a bowl, cream the butter and sugar. Add the syrup and stir until light and fluffy. Mix in the flour until the texture is such that you are able to roll into tablespoon-sized balls. Place on a baking tray lined with baking paper, 2cm apart, and press each gently with a fork. Bake for 12 to 15 minutes or until golden. Cool completely before eating.

Lunchbox Tip: These are lovely in a lunchbox and pressed together gently with a little hazelnut spread … Deeeelicioso.

Why did the Cookie go to the Doctor?

It was feeling crummy!!!

Chocolate Coated Ritz

f *Our Foodie Family quickly named these 'The After School Ritz Blitz!'*

Makes 18

- *100g dark chocolate*
- *18 Ritz Crackers*
- *2 tablespoons peanut butter*

In a microwave safe bowl, break the chocolate and melt on high checking every 30 seconds, until the chocolate is nice and smooth. Take 8 crackers and dip each half way into the chocolate. Gently shake to remove excess chocolate. With the remaining crackers sandwich two together with peanut butter and dip into the chocolate, turning to completely coat. Again, gently shake to remove excess chocolate. Refrigerate for 30 minutes or until the chocolate is set.

F.A.M.I.L.Y = **F**ather **A**nd **M**other **I** **L**ove **Y**ou!

Dinosaur Eggs

Once upon a time when I was making these in my kitchen, my beautiful then 5 year old walked up to me, looked quizzically and said "Mum they look like Dinosaur Eggs!" No longer were they Apricot Balls, but forever more Dinosaur Eggs!

Makes 40

- *2½ cups (300g) desiccated coconut (or shredded to roll)*
- *400g dried apricots, finely chopped*
- *400g can condensed milk*

Measure out ½ cup coconut and set aside on a wide, flat plate. Place the remaining coconut in a bowl and stir in the apricots and condensed milk. With wet hands, roll 2 teaspoons of mixture into a 'dinosaur egg' and roll in the reserved coconut. Refrigerate or freeze for a later date.

Dot 2 Dot Cookies

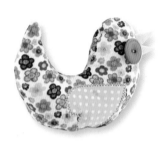

Just try and stop at 1 ... or 2!

Makes 24

- 500g packet Devil's food cake mix
- ½ cup (115g) butter, melted
- 2 eggs
- 100g Smarties

Preheat the oven to 180°C. In a large bowl, combine the cake mix, butter, and eggs and stir until combined. Line two baking trays with baking paper. Using a tablespoon, dollop a spoonful of mixture onto the baking trays, 3 to 4cm apart to allow for spreading. Gently press with a fork and top each with four Smarties. Bake for 10 minutes. Remove from the oven and allow to cool and harden.

Edible Veggie Bowl & Dip

Serves 4

- *1 red capsicum (pepper)*
- *450g butternut pumpkin, peeled*
- *½ cup (80g) cashews*
- *3 tablespoons grated Parmesan cheese*

Preheat oven to 180°C. Cut the pumpkin into 4cm cubes, place onto a baking tray and roast for 20 minutes or until golden in colour and soft in texture. Allow to cool for 15 minutes, then place the roasted pumpkin, cashew nuts and Parmesan cheese into a food processor and blend until combined. Season to taste. While chilling in the fridge, halve the capsicum and remove its seeds and membrane. Keeping one half as your 'edible bowl' cut the other half into dipping sticks. Spoon the dip into the bowls, and then add the dippers to decorate. I chose to use them to create a thick sweep of eyelashes (I used some carrot and celery too). My little boys were mighty impressed!

 Keep nutrition fun so kids will enjoy being healthy. Try to be creative, for example, a slice of carrot may be met with more enthusiasm when called a "carrot chip."

Grape Wands

Makes 12

- *200g green grapes*
- *200g red grapes*
- *12 medium kebab sticks*

Onto the sticks thread the grapes. For visual effect, vary the colour pattern by using just green or just red, alternate colours, or use three green and top with three red! At my 6 year old's birthday party last year these were among the first to be eaten!

JOKE – What do you get if you cross a chicken with a cement mixer?

A bricklayer!

M&M Bars

Jasmine Jones wrote, "I can't begin to thank you enough for this recipe, my kids just love it, they are a lunchbox staple in our house."

Makes 16

- *220g packet Arrowroot biscuits (Hobnobs, Graeme Crackers)*
- *400g can condensed milk*
- *1 cup M&Ms*

Preheat the oven to 160°C. Line a 8 x 25cm bar tray with baking paper. Process the cookies in a blender or food processor to fine crumbs, then pour into a large bowl. Add the remaining ingredients and combine well. Scrape the mixture into the prepared tray. Bake for 20 minutes. Let cool, then cut into 16 scrum-diddily-umptious bars.

Kaywana Brunello substituted arrowroot biscuits for Chocolate Ripple which I thought was really clever!

Play Date Buddies

Makes 2

- *75g white grapes*
- *75g red grapes*
- *¼ cup popcorn*
- *8 pretzels*

Into two zip-lock snack bags place the grapes in one side and the popcorn and pretzels on the other. Using a wooden peg, clamp it down the centre and decorate it as you want. These are a fun addition to any lunchbox, mix it up with whatever healthy snacks your kids will eat!

Optional: Fill with healthy snacks such as dried fruit, fresh whole fruit like grapes or berries, popcorn, cereal or crackers. These also make gorgeous party bags filled with sweet treats.

Tip: To make these you will also need a few crafty bits 'n' bobs; wooden clothes pegs, coloured pipe cleaners, paint and stick on googly eyes (or you can draw your own on).
I also use these 'Buddies' to hang my boy's artwork from a piece of string in their bedrooms.

Taco Popcorn

Serves 6 to 8

- *8 cups (320g) popped popcorn*
- *3 tablespoons (45g) butter, melted*
- *2 teaspoons taco seasoning mix*

Place the popcorn in a large bowl. In a small bowl, mix together the butter and taco seasoning (start with 1 teaspoon and taste before adding more). Drizzle over the popcorn and toss to coat thoroughly. Serve immediately.

Optional: To make a delicious BBQ Popcorn; to 2 tablespoons of melted butter, add ½ teaspoon chilli powder, ½ teaspoon garlic salt, ¼ teaspoon onion powder and mix in 8 cups freshly popped popcorn. Serve sprinkled with finely grated Parmesan cheese.

Tickled Pink

I love smoothies, as they are a quick and an easy way to add a variety of fruit to your kids diet.

Makes 2

- *4 cups cold watermelon*
- *2 cups frozen strawberries*
- *½ cup (125g) fruit yoghurt*
- *1 cup crushed ice*

Pop all ingredients into a blender and blend until smooth.

Optional: Banana & raspberries make a nice team, as does 1 frozen banana, 5 frozen strawberries, the juice of 1 orange and 1 cup soya milk … Deeeeelish!

What's 4 Lunch?

BABY BLTS

f Becky Butler, "they make a lovely lunch."

Makes 12

- *12 dinner rolls*
- *6 slices bacon, halved*
- *¼ head iceberg lettuce, shredded*
- *2 small tomatoes, thinly sliced*

Preheat the oven to 180°C. Place the rolls on a baking paper lined baking tray and cut horizontally without cutting all the way through. Bake for 5 minutes or until just crunchy. Meanwhile, in a large frying pan, cook the bacon until crisp. Drain on paper towels. Just before serving, fill the rolls with bacon, lettuce, and tomato.

Optional: Brush inside the rolls with mayonnaise or barbecue sauce before filling.
And to create your own 'BLAT' add a fresh slice of creamy avocado.

Chicken & Spinach Rolls

This recipe was shared by the Junior Squad of Golf Queensland … Rising superstars on the course and in the kitchen!

Makes 12

- *400g chicken mince*
- *75g baby spinach*
- *225g can creamed corn*
- *2 sheets shortcrust pastry*

Preheat the oven to 200°C. Line a baking tray with baking paper. In a large nonstick frying pan, cook the mince over high heat until cooked through, 4 minutes. Let cool, then stir in the spinach and corn, and season to taste. Halve the pastry, spoon a quarter of the chicken mixture down the long edge of one piece of pastry. Roll to enclose the filling and cut into three pieces. Gently score the surface of each 3 to 4 times. Repeat with the remaining pieces of pastry and chicken mixture. Place the rolls on the baking tray and bake until browned, about 30 minutes.

Optional: Brush with a beaten egg before baking for a glistening shine.

 Grated zucchini (courgette), carrot and Spanish onion is also nice in these.

Chicken Calypso Sambo

Transform the humble sandwich into a lunchbox favourite.

Makes 2

- *½ cup shredded cooked chicken*
- *4 dried apricots, finely diced*
- *2 tablespoons mayonnaise*
- *2 slices multigrain bread*

In a bowl, mix together the chicken, apricots, and mayonnaise. Use as a sandwich filling for the two slices of bread. Slice the sandwich before serving or wrap tightly and pop it into a lunchbox.

 Add a lettuce leaf for colour and crunch and serve in a lunchbox with our Purple Pancakes (p. 26).

Cinderella's Pumpkin Soup

Anastasia and Drizella will be envious of this soup too!

Serves 4

- *1 tablespoon butter*
- *1 leek (white part only), washed and sliced*
- *250g pumpkin or butternut squash, peeled and cut into cubes*
- *2 cups (500ml) vegetable stock*

In a saucepan, melt the butter. Add the leek and sauté until soft and lightly golden. Add the pumpkin and cook for 2 minutes. Add the stock and bring to a boil. Reduce to a simmer, cover, and cook until the pumpkin is tender, about 30 minutes. Allow the soup to cool slightly before pouring it into the blender. Blend until nice and smooth.

This soup is equally delicious adding chopped onions, potatoes, corn, garlic and spices like ground coriander, cumin and nutmeg.

Fancy Fingers

Serves 2

- *6 slices bread, crusts removed*
- *2 slices cheese*
- *2 slices ham*
- *½ cup shredded lettuce*

Onto two slices of bread, place a slice of cheese and ham. Cover with another piece of bread, add lettuce and top with final slice of bread. Cut into thirds and stack on each other to serve.

 Use fillings with different textures; a little softened cream cheese and stir into it salmon and dill, boiled eggs mashed with a little mayonnaise, grated cheese and chutney, cottage cheese with sultanas, spring onions or pineapple all make delicious fillings for such 'fingers'.

Healthy Omelette

Serves 2

- *3 eggs*
- *½ cup grated cheddar cheese*
- *1 teaspoon freshly chopped parsley*
- *1 tablespoon butter*

In a bowl, beat the eggs. Whisk in 3 tablespoons of cold water, the cheese and parsley into the eggs. In a nonstick frying pan, over medium heat, melt the butter. When foaming, pour in the egg mixture. Reduce the heat to low and cook for 3 to 4 minutes or until the mixture looks set and is golden underneath. Use a spatula to carefully fold one side of the omelette over the filling. Cut the omelette into pieces or serve whole.

Serve with a simple salad of baby spinach, fresh mint and toasted almonds.

Tip: The real secret to a perfectly cooked omelette is to cook it over a LOW heat. If the heat is too high the base will burn whilst the middle is still runny. For best results use a 20 to 24cm high quality nonstick flat pan, see www.4ingredients.com.au

Hot-Diggety Dogs

Makes 4

- *4 hot dogs (frankfurters)*
- *400g can baked beans*
- *4 long hot dog buns*
- *½ cup grated cheddar cheese*

In a saucepan of simmering water, cook the hot dogs for 5 to 7 minutes. Meanwhile, in a small saucepan, warm the baked beans. Place the drained hot dogs in the buns and top with the baked beans and cheese.

 There are many possible fillings for Hot-Diggety Dogs; make a quick salsa from tomatoes, red capsicum (peppers) and coriander, caramelized onions, bacon, cheese and onions or simply serve with the classic tomato sauce and mustard.

jOkE – How do you get straight A's?

Use a ruler!!!!

Lunch Box Sushi

Serves 2

- *4 slices soy and linseed bread*
- *1 tablespoon whole egg mayonnaise*
- *½ avocado, mashed*
- *½ cucumber, thinly sliced*

Remove the crusts from the slices of bread. Along the middle of each slice spread a little mayonnaise and avocado. Place long, thin strips of cucumber on top and roll tightly. Cut in thirds, turn up and place tightly into the lunchbox, with seams touching each other so as not to fall apart.

Use a variety fillings; asparagus, boiled eggs, carrot, cucumber, enoki mushrooms, radish and add a dash of lemon juice to keep fresh and green.

Here are some of my favourite suggestions:

Avocado, shredded chicken and thin slices of cheese • Cream cheese, salmon and thin slices of cucumber • Cottage cheese, thinly sliced carrot and sultanas • Curried egg • Egg and lettuce • Grated apple, sultanas and cream cheese • Ham, cheese and finely shredded lettuce • Peanut butter and thinly sliced carrot • Tuna, mayonnaise and finely shredded lettuce • Vegemite and thin slices of cheese.

Pizzadilla

Serves 4

- *4 whole wheat tortillas*
- *50g English spinach*
- *⅔ cup grated mozzarella cheese*
- *1 cup (175g) pasta sauce*

Divide the spinach and mozzarella between two of the tortillas. Top with the remaining tortillas. Place a nonstick frying pan over medium heat. Gently slide 1 pizzadilla into the pan and cook until golden on the base, about 2 minutes. Using a spatula, gently flip and cook the other side until the cheese melts, 1 to 2 minutes. Transfer the pizzadilla to a cutting board. Repeat with second pizzadilla. Cut both pizzadillas into wedges. Serve with the warmed pasta sauce for dipping.

 I LOVE these for veggie smuggling, grate in any number of extra veggies as it's the melted cheese and pasta sauce for dipping that the kids love most. I'd recommend; mashed kidney beans, avocado, finely chopped red capsicum (pepper), corn and onions.

Quiche Cakes

(for a Lady Bugs Picnic)

---

f *Thank you Ava Roberts, 7 for naming these divine little quiches.*

Makes 12

- *1 sheet short crust pastry*
- *¼ cup (70g) tomato sauce*
- *4 eggs, beaten*
- *½ cup grated cheese*

Preheat oven 180°C. Using a 5.5cm scalloped-edge scone cutter cut 12 rounds from the short crust pastry. Gently press each into a nonstick 12-holed cupcake (fairy cake / patty cake) tray. Brush each with tomato sauce. Add half the cheese to the beaten eggs and season to taste, mix well before spooning the mixture evenly among the 12 cups. Sprinkle each with the remaining cheese. Bake for 12 minutes or until golden and cooked through.

Quiches are a superb vehicle to smuggle veggies, literally the sky is the limit! Spinach and broccoli precooked, roast pumpkin cubes drizzled with olive oil and chilli flakes, sliced mushroom, tomatoes and onions sprinkled with Parmesan cheese, Antipasto mix are all yum-scrum combinations.

Sandwich Rollups

Makes 12

- *4 slices brown bread*
- *1 tablespoon butter*
- *Sandwich fillings; ham, cheese, pastrami, spreads*
- *1 bunch of chives*

Remove the crusts from the bread. Lay each slice onto a clean, flat surface and with a rolling pin, roll out until each slice is quite thin. Butter lightly and top each with your chosen filling(s). Roll tightly, cut into thirds and tie with a chive.

A good lunch box should provide your children with enough energy to sustain them all afternoon. Use fillings rich in protein; chicken, cheese, ham and tuna and loaded with vitamins and minerals; green leafy lettuce leaves, grated carrot and finely sliced cucumber. Use different types of bread and wraps and cut into triangles, squares, fingers or roll as above and secure with a straight pretzel sword (Oh! I meant stick!)

Spaghetti Cupcakes

Hailey Earnshaw wrote, "OMG why have I not found your page earlier!? My two tots can be the fussiest of eaters. Tonight I made the Spaghetti Cupcakes and they are scoffing them down!"

Makes 12

- *Olive oil spray*
- *4 eggs, beaten*
- *2 cups grated mozzarella cheese*
- *400g can spaghetti*

Preheat the oven to 180°C. Lightly grease 12 cups of a muffin tin with olive oil spray. In a bowl, beat the eggs. Add 1½ cups of the cheese and the spaghetti and stir to combine. Using a quarter-cup measure, divide the mixture evenly among the muffin cups. Sprinkle each with the remaining cheese. Bake until the eggs are set and the cheese is lightly browned, about 15 minutes.

These 'Cupcakes' can easily be decorated with sliced olives, mushrooms, ham, or red capsicum (peppers) or baked with grated zucchini (courgette), carrot, onions and corn included.

You **Tube** *4 Ingredients Channel / Spaghetti Cupcakes*

Zucchini Slice

Serves 4

- 6 eggs
- 1 cup grated zucchini (courgette)
- ½ cup (90g) self-raising flour
- 1 cup grated cheddar cheese

Preheat oven to 180°C. Line a 20 x 30cm baking tray with baking paper. In a large bowl, whisk the eggs, add the remaining ingredients and season to taste. Pour the contents into the prepared tray and bake for 25 minutes or until nice and brown. Allow to cool slightly, then serve sliced with a simple little salad.

Grate into this onion, carrot, corn or sauté a little leek or bacon.
Remember these are lovely served cold in the lunchbox.

jOkE - What's the world's strongest vegetable?

Muscle Sprouts!

What's 4 Dinner?

5-Minute Fettuccine Carbonara

Serves 4

- *350g fettuccine*
- *4 slices bacon, chopped*
- *3 eggs, beaten*
- *¾ cup grated Parmesan cheese*

Cook the pasta according to package directions. Meanwhile, in a frying pan, cook the bacon until crisp. Drain on paper towels. In a bowl, mix together the eggs and cheese. Drain the pasta well and add it to the egg mixture, tossing to coat the pasta well. Add the bacon and toss again. Serve immediately.

 Add ½ cup of peas to the fettuccine in the last 1 to 2 minutes of boiling and cook together for some nutritious greens with dinner.

Dine as a family. Dinner together makes a difference.

Beef & Plum Stir-fry

f Kim Bertuzzi wrote, "This is an absolute divine creamy beef stir-fry, without the cream!"

Serves 4 ❄

- ½ cup (140g) plum sauce
- 1 tablespoon English mustard
- 500g beef stir-fry
- 1 cup (170g) sultanas

In a frying pan, combine the plum sauce, mustard, and ½ cup water and bring to a boil. Add the beef and cook over a high heat for 8 minutes. Add the raisins and cook for another 2 minutes.

 Add thin strips of capsicum (pepper) or spring onions to the stir-fry and serve over rice … What could be simpler?

Beef Stroganoff

Daddy makes this all the time, quick, easy and tasty.

Serves 4

- *500g beef stir-fry*
- *1 packet (40g) beef Stroganoff seasoning*
- *200g cream cheese, softened*
- *200g mushrooms, sliced*

Heat a nonstick frying pan and lightly brown the beef. Add the seasoning with ½ cup (125ml) water and simmer gently for 30 minutes. Add the cream cheese, and stir until it forms part of the creamy gravy-like sauce. Add the mushrooms and simmer for a further 5 minutes or until the mushrooms are soft and tender.

Serve over rice to soak up the deliciously rich and inviting sauce and with your kids favourite veggies like asparagus and carrot! Garnish with some sliced spring onions.

Easy Peasy Fish Cakes

A recipe from the lovely Robyn Mayeke.

Makes 8

- *1 cup cooked, flaked fish*
- *1 cup mashed potato*
- *½ cup fresh or frozen peas*
- *1 egg*

Simply mix altogether, season and roll into balls. Chill for 30 minutes before heating a nonstick frying pan over medium heat and lightly frying. Cook for 3 minutes one side, then flip and cook for the same on the other side.

 Add a variety of herbs and veggies into such savoury cakes; grated carrot, finely chopped spring onions, a little lemon zest, chopped parsley and corn kernels are some of my favourites ☺

Echidna Balls

When baking, the rice expands and will pop out of the meatballs,
this is what makes them look like echidnas!

Serves 6

- *800g beef mince*
- *2 eggs, beaten*
- *1 cup cooked long-grain white rice*
- *2 x 400g cans condensed tomato soup*

Preheat the oven to 180°C. In a bowl, combine the beef, eggs, rice and season with sea salt and pepper to taste. Mix well and form into 4cm diameter meatballs. Place in a large baking dish and cover with the soup. Take each can and swirl ¼ cup water water in it, add this liquid to the meatballs. Bake for 50 minutes or until the mince is cooked through.

 Serve with mashed potato and steamed veggies like broccoli and carrot and
for extra veggie content add grated carrot and zucchini to the mince mixture.

The nicest thing you can wear is a smile.

Grandma

Mac 'n' Cheese

This is a timeless classic. Kids, big and small around the world like Mac 'n' Cheese!

Serves 4 to 6

- *1 cup grated cheddar cheese*
- *4 cups cooked elbow macaroni*
- *500ml cream*
- *2 eggs, beaten*

Preheat the oven to 160°C. Measure out ¼ cup of the cheddar and set aside. In a bowl, combine the remaining cheddar, macaroni, cream, and eggs; season with sea salt and pepper. Mix well and pour into a 20cm baking dish and bake until the sauce thickens, 35 to 40 minutes.

 Mixing through some peas, corn and carrot finely diced, never hurt anyone!

You Tube *4 Ingredients Channel / Mac 'n' Cheese*

Meatloaf Cupcakes

Makes 12

- *500g beef mince*
- *1 egg*
- *2 slices multigrain bread, grated*
- *¼ cup (70g) BBQ sauce, plus extra for basting*

Preheat the oven to 180°C. In a large bowl, combine the mince, egg, bread, and BBQ sauce. Divide the mixture evenly among the muffin cups. Brush the tops with a little more sauce and bake until cooked through, about 20 to 25 minutes. Remove from oven and rest.

Optional: For the 'icing' spoon warm, leftover mashed potato into a ziploc bag. Cut a small edge off the corner and pipe the potato onto the top of each meatloaf in a swirling motion to make your 'cupcakes.'

 The options are endless but some of my favourite smuggling ideas are; finely chopped celery, onion, grated carrot and beetroot, and seasoned with fresh thyme.

Mexican Enchiladas

Enchilada literally means "enchilied" in this case dipped in chili sauce, choose a mild Enchilada Sauce if you are making this for your kids for the first time.

Makes 10

- *12 x 20cm tortillas*
- *2 cups shredded roast chicken*
- *275g jar enchilada sauce*
- *1½ cups grated mozzarella cheese*

Preheat the oven to 180°C. Warm the tortillas in the microwave for 30 seconds or until soft. Meanwhile in a bowl, add the chicken, ¾ of the sauce and one cup of cheese and stir to combine. Divide the mixture among the tortillas, roll up and place in a baking dish seam-side down. Drizzle the remaining sauce across the top the tortillas and sprinkle with remaining mozzarella. Bake until golden, about 20 to 25 minutes.

 These are the perfect veggie smuggler as the kids can't see what you add into them. Smashed kidney or pinto beans, chopped tomatoes, onions, garlic or diced olives all blend beautifully.

Popeye's Pie

When I first served this to my kids I encouraged them to try it by telling them about Popeye, Olive Oyl and poor old Bluto … They quizzically looked at me and asked "Who are they????"

Serves 8 ❄

- *1 sheet puff pastry*
- *3 eggs*
- *250g ricotta cheese*
- *70g spinach*

Preheat oven 180°C. Line a 23cm quiche dish with baking paper. Lay onto it the pastry. In a bowl, whisk the eggs, add the ricotta and mix well. Add the spinach and season to taste. Pour the mixture into the pastry and bake for 25 to 30 minutes or until set.

 Pies and Quiches are a great way to hide veggies; onion, garlic, oregano, corn and pinenuts are a great addition to this pie.

Quick 'n' Easy Pasta Bake

Serves 4

- *350g cheese tortellini*
- *500g jar pasta sauce*
- *½ cup basil leaves*
- *1 cup shredded mozzarella cheese*

Preheat the oven to 180°C. Cook the tortellini according to package directions. Drain and toss with the pasta sauce, basil and half the cheese. Season to taste. Pour the mixture into a baking dish and sprinkle with the remaining mozzarella. Bake until the cheese is golden brown and bubbling, 15 to 20 minutes.

Make a puree from any of these individually or combined; pumpkin, sweet potato, Swede, parsnip and carrot and add this to the pasta sauce … It's very very nice and the kids seldom realize what they are eating.

Sammy Salmon Pasta

Serves 2

- *4 broccoli florets, quartered*
- *½ cup (125ml) cream*
- *200g salmon fillet, grilled and broken up into small pieces*
- *100g angel hair pasta, cooked*

Heat a nonstick frying pan. Bring ½ cup (125ml) water to the boil. Add the broccoli and cook for 4 minutes or until tender, drain well. To it, add the cream and gently stir. Stir in salmon and mix until heated through. Add the pasta and toss to combine.

f *Here is another really simple 'kid friendly' salmon recipe; marinate salmon in teriyaki sauce in the fridge for at least 2 hours. In a lightly oiled baking dish, place the salmon, drizzle with teriyaki marinade, and sprinkle with a teaspoon of brown sugar (1 teaspoon sugar for each salmon steak). Bake in a 180°C oven for 30 minutes or until the salmon flakes easily. Spoon the pan jus over the salmon to serve.*

Sticky Lamb Chops

These are a great way to ease your kids on into spicier foods, increase or decrease the sweet chilli sauce as much as you think they'd like.

Serves 4

- *2 tablespoons soy sauce*
- *3 tablespoons sweet chilli sauce*
- *8 lamb chops*

Mix soy and sweet chili sauces. Preheat a BBQ or grill to high and cook the chops for 2 minutes on each side. Reduce the heat to medium and continue cooking for 2 to 3 minutes while brushing with the tasty baste. Cover loosely with foil and allow to rest for 5 minutes before serving.

Optional: Serve with creamy mashed potato, corn on the cob and peas.

Sweet Chicken Fingers

This recipe came from a nutritionist, Cyndi O'Meara ... They are sensational!

Serves 6

- *1 kg chicken tenderloins*
- *¾ cup (185g) natural yoghurt*
- *2 cups (240g) cornflakes, crushed*
- *1 cup grated Parmesan cheese*

Preheat the oven to 180°C. Line a baking tray with baking paper. In a shallow bowl, combine the cornflakes and Parmesan. Place yoghurt in a second shallow bowl. Coat the chicken with the yoghurt and then roll in the cornflake mixture. Place on the baking tray. Bake for 15 minutes, or until the chicken is cooked through and the crumbing golden and crunchy.

 Serve this with potato salad and sweet corn on the cob or mashed potato, peas and roasted cherry tomatoes.

Tempura Fish Bites

Kids generally love 'bite-size' anything.

Makes 16

- *500g white fish fillets*
- *1 cup (120g) cornflour*
- *1 egg*
- *½ cup (125ml) vegetable oil*

Cut the fish into 2cm cubes (you should have about 16). Pop the cornflour into a medium bowl. Stir in the egg and ¾ cup (185ml) of really cold water until just combined. Let the batter stand for a few minutes. In a large frying pan or wok, heat the oil until shimmering, but not smoking. Dip the fish cubes in the batter, allowing excess to drip off. Working in batches (so as not to overcrowd the pan), cook the fish until the batter is very lightly browned and the fish turns white and is cooked through.

Optional: Add 1 tablespoon lemon juice to the batter to create yummy 'Lemony Fish Bites' and substitute really cold seltzer or soda water for the water if you have any.

Tomato Drummies

Easy and Economical!

Serves 4

- *1 kg chicken drumsticks*
- *420g can condensed tomato soup*
- *1 packet (40g) French onion soup*

Preheat oven to 180°C. Place the chicken legs in a 24cm square ovenproof dish. Stir together the tomato soup, onion soup mix, and half a cup of water and pour over the chicken legs. Bake for 1 hour or until the chicken is cooked through.

 Serve with mashed potatoes or cauliflower and steamed beans and zucchini.

Homemade Takeaway

3-Cheese Pizza

One of my personal favourite Pizza recipes.

Makes 2

- *100g mozzarella cheese, shredded*
- *100g feta cheese, crumbled*
- *½ cup grated Parmesan cheese*
- *2 ready-made pizza bases*

Preheat the oven to 200°C. Divide the three cheeses between the bases. Bake until the cheeses melt and the bases are crisp, 10 to 12 minutes. Let cool slightly, then cut into wedges to serve.

Top with a tasty Guacamole; take 1 avocado, mash and add to it 1 tablespoon each of chopped red onion and coriander and 1 teaspoon of lime juice.

Beef & Veggie Pies

f *Rebecca Leeson, "These are one of my kids' favourite meals!"*

Makes 12 ❄

- *500g beef mince*
- *2 cups frozen mixed vegetables, thawed*
- *495g jar pasta sauce*
- *4 sheets puff pastry*

Preheat the oven to 200°C. In a nonstick frying pan, brown the beef. Add the veggies and season with sea salt and pepper to taste. Pour in the sauce and simmer for 10 minutes. Meanwhile, cut 24 x 6cm circles from the puff pastry. Line 12 cups of a nonstick muffin tin with 12 pastry rounds. Divide the beef mixture among the muffin cups and top with the remaining rounds of pastry. Seal the edges with a fork, sprinkle with pepper and pierce once with a knife to create a vent. Bake until the pastry is nice and golden, about 20 minutes.

Pies are a terrific way to hide veggies. For the fussiest of eaters you can even puree roasted pumpkin, sweet potato or parsnips and add to the pasta sauce. They'll never ever know ☺

Chicken Nuggets

f *Kay 'Apples' Smith, "I make these every single week, some weeks we have with salad, some weeks with veggies."*

Serves 2 ❄

- *2 chicken breast halves, cut into bite-size pieces*
- *1 cup (260g) mayonnaise*
- *1 cup (130g) bread crumbs*
- *1 tablespoon butter, melted*

Preheat the oven to 180°C. Line a baking tray with baking paper. Coat the chicken with the mayonnaise and roll in the breadcrumbs. Place on the baking tray. Drizzle with the butter and bake for 15 to 20 minutes or until golden.

Hamburger

Serves 4 ❄

- *500g beef mince*
- *200g bacon, finely diced*
- *1 cup grated cheddar cheese*
- *½ cup (140g) BBQ sauce*

Line a baking tray with greaseproof paper. In a large bowl, combine the beef, bacon, cheese, BBQ sauce, and sea salt and pepper to taste and mix well. Form into 4 patties; 10cm in diameter and 1.5cm thick. Place the patties onto the tray. Cover with cling film and place in the fridge for at least 30 minutes to rest. Chilling the patties will help them hold together when cooking. In a large nonstick frying pan cook each pattie for 4 minutes on each side or until cooked through.

 Add 1 tablespoon chopped fresh parsley to the mix. Parsley is very high in vitamin C, so add it to meals whenever you can. Serve with a slice of yummy pineapple, tomato and fresh, crispy lettuce. And for a really nice Turkey Burger, mix 500g turkey mince, 1 small onion, diced, 1 green apple, grated and 1 egg. Mix, form into patties, chill then grill!

Healthy Fish 'n' Chips

Serves 4

- *500g firm white fish fillets*
- *2 slices whole grain bread, grated*
- *¾ teaspoon All-purpose seasoning*
- *1 egg, beaten*

Preheat oven to 180°C. Line a baking tray with baking paper. Pat the fish dry and cut into 3cm-wide strips. Combine the breadcrumbs and seasoning on a plate. Coat one piece of fish in the egg, then in the breadcrumbs. Place on the prepared tray and repeat with remaining ingredients. Cook for 10 to 15 minutes, turning halfway through.

Serve with sweet potato fries; peel and slice the sweet potato into 1cm long and wide slices. In a large bowl, toss with just enough oil to coat and season. Spread in single layer on a baking tray and bake in a preheated 180°C oven for 15 to 20 minutes or until tender.

jOkE – What do whales eat for dinner?

Fish & ships!

Pizza

 This is one of the best veggie smuggling meals I know. I've even sliced brussels sprouts on it and watched it be gobbled up!

Makes 2

- *3 slices bacon, finely diced*
- *4 tablespoons pizza sauce*
- *2 pita breads*
- *½ cup grated mozzarella cheese*

Preheat the grill in your oven to 180°C. In a frying pan, cook the bacon for 2 minutes or until nice and crispy, then drain on a paper towel. Spread the pizza sauce on the pita bread, sprinkle with the bacon, and top with the mozzarella. Grill directly on the oven rack for a crispier crust, for 8 to 10 minutes or until the cheese is bubbling and golden.

Veggie Ribbon Pasta

Serves 4

- *1 zucchini*
- *1 carrot*
- *1 parsnip*
- *400g jar of your favourite pasta sauce*

Wash the veggies and peel the carrot and parsnip. Take a veggie peeler and make ribbons out of each. Bring a medium saucepan of salted water to the boil. Add the veggie ribbons and boil for 3 minutes. Remove and drain. Pop into a large nonstick frying pan and season. Pour in pasta sauce and simmer until warmed through. Serve immediately.

Optional: Serve sprinkled with Parmesan cheese and garnish with fresh basil.

Wok-On

Serves 4

- *8 sausages, casings removed*
- *250g egg noodles*
- *¼ cup (60ml) tamari soy sauce*
- *2 tablespoons honey*

Preheat the oven to 180°C. Line a baking tray with baking paper. Using 'little hands' roll the sausage meat into meatballs and place on the baking tray. Bake until golden brown, 10 to 12 minutes. Meanwhile, cook the noodles according to package directions. In a small bowl, combine the tamari and honey. Drain the noodles and transfer to a large nonstick wok. Add the meatballs and sauce and over a medium heat, toss thoroughly before serving.

 OK the gloves come off in a stir-fry, these are what vegetables were made for!
Add a variety of freshly sliced or cubed vegetables for colour and nutrition.

What's 4 Dessert?

4-Minute Strawberry Soft Serve

I don't have an ice-cream machine, so for me this recipe is brilliant!

Serves 4 ❄

- *275g frozen strawberries*
- *¼ cup (50g) caster sugar*
- *⅔ cup (160ml) cream*
- *¼ teaspoon vanilla*

Combine the frozen strawberries and sugar in a food processor or blender. Process until the fruit is roughly chopped. Add the cream and vanilla and blend until combined. Serve immediately as a delectable soft serve, or freeze for at least 4 hours for a nice firm ice-cream.

Optional: The flavours for this are endless; raspberry, mango, blueberries and for a lighter version, substitute cream for your kid's favourite yoghurt.

90-Second Microwave Fudge

"This is the best fudge I've ever tasted", Connor 8.

Makes 16

- *250g dark chocolate, broken up*
- *400g can condensed milk*
- *1 cup (120g) chopped walnuts*

Line an 18cm square cake pan with baking paper. In a large microwaveable bowl, melt the chocolate in 30-second increments, stirring after each, until smooth and creamy. Gradually add the condensed milk, stirring all the while. Add the nuts and stir to combine. Spread the mixture in the cake pan and refrigerate for 1 hour or until set. Cut into 16 squares.

Tip: All nuts are an important component of the healthy eating pyramid. The special thing about walnuts is that they not only look like our wrinkled brains but they are very good for our wrinkled brains, as they are high in omega-3 fat.

You Tube *4 Ingredients Channel / Microwave Fudge*

Banana Splitz

This recipe is how my kid's like to eat Banana Splitz, none are fans of maraschino cherries nor whipped cream ... You make this however your kids like it!

Makes 4

- *4 bananas*
- *16 marshmallows*
- *4 scoops creamy vanilla ice-cream*
- *½ cup strawberry sauce / topping*

Peel the bananas and lay each into four serving plates. Dot each with 4 marshmallows, dollop with ice-cream and drizzle with strawberry sauce.

Optional: If serving as dessert at a party, add wafers and M&Ms for a real burst of colour. Alternatively, substitute strawberry sauce with your own homemade chocolate sauce; in a small saucepan over low heat, melt 100g of butter, add ½ cup (110g) brown sugar, ½ cup (125ml) cream and 2 tablespoons of cocoa powder and stir for 3 minutes or until well combined. Cool a little prior to serving.

Caramel Cupcakes

Submitted through facebook by Cassandra Van Breugal and is INCREDIBLY POPULAR!

Makes 24

- *1 cup (175g) self-raising flour*
- *400g can Top n Fill or Carnation Caramel*
- *1 egg*
- *⅓ cup (75g) butter, at room temperature*

Preheat the oven to 180°C. Sift the flour into a bowl and add the caramel, egg, and butter. With an electric mixer, beat until pale and fluffy, about 2 minutes. Line 24 mini muffin cups with paper liners. Divide the batter among the cups and bake until light golden brown, about 10 minutes.

Optional: For a dazzling finish, top with a simple ganache, made by warming 1 cup (250ml) of cream and adding 250g dark chocolate to it, stirring until it combines.
To top, garnish with a slice of Mars Bar.

Heaven in a Cookie

These are S.E.N.S.A.T.I.O.N.A.L

Makes 18

- *500g vanilla ice-cream, softened*
- *⅔ cup crunchy peanut butter*
- *200g packet crunchy chocolate biscuits*

In a large bowl, beat the ice-cream and peanut butter with an electric mixer until nice and smooth. Pour the mixture back into the vanilla ice-cream tub and freeze. Meanwhile, take each biscuit and place them flat side up onto the tops of your cupcake (patty cake / fairy cake) tins. Pop them into a preheated 180°C oven for 5 minutes or until soft to touch. Remove from the oven, then carefully press each of the biscuits into the cupcake mold. Let them sit to cool. When ready to serve, dollop a scoop of the deliciously creamy peanut butter ice-cream into each biscuit 'cup'.

Optional: Serve drizzled with Hot Fudge Sauce (see Tip on page 148).

Jelly Cocktails

 Recipe from Linda Kruger ... Thank you, these are AMAZING!

Makes 20

- *3 packets (75g) raspberry jelly crystals*
- *1 sachet (10g) gelatin*
- *1 cup (250ml) cream*

In a heatproof jug, stir together the jelly crystals and gelatin. Add 3 cups (750ml) boiling water and stir until the gelatin is dissolved. Cool for 5 minutes then stir in the cream. Pour into 20 cocktail cups or a baking paper lined a 24 x 30cm baking pan and refrigerate until set, at least 4 hours.

Optional: Garnish with 'Rose Petal Chips'. Onto a paper lined baking tray lay the petals from a rose. Brush lightly with egg white and sprinkle with caster sugar. Leave overnight to dry.

You Tube *4 Ingredients Channel / Jelly Slice*

Mars Bar Slice

Y.U.M - Y.U.M - Y.U.M!

Serves 6

- *2 x 53g Mars Bars, chopped*
- *¾ cup (170g) butter*
- *3 cups (240g) Rice Bubbles*

Line a 20 x 30cm baking pan with baking paper. Then in a microwave safe dish, melt the Mar Bars and butter on high, in 30-second increments, stirring each time until the mixture is quite smooth. Add the rice bubbles and mix well. Press into the prepared tray. Refrigerate for 1 hour or until set, then cut into slices when ready to serve.

There are no seven wonders of the world in the eyes of a child.
There are SEVEN MILLION!

Walt Streightiff

Sensational Sundae

Serves 4

- *8 scoops creamy, choc-chip ice-cream*
- *1 cup (120g) hazelnuts, chopped*
- *½ cup choc hazelnut spread*
- *2 Flake chocolate bars*

Layer four serving glasses with ice-cream, hazelnuts and the spread. Top with half a chocolate flake on each, serve immediately!

Optional: Try my Aunt's famous Chocolate Fudge Sundae; in a saucepan over low heat melt 1 can condensed milk with 100g dark chocolate, stirring for 3 minutes or until nice and smooth. Cool slightly. Into 4 serving glasses place a scoop of vanilla ice-cream and drizzle each with half the chocolate fudge sauce. Continue layering. Put a scoop of vanilla ice-cream into 4 serving glasses and drizzle each with half of the chocolate fudge sauce.

"You can never be too full for dessert."

Kelly, age 4

Toblerone Slice

f *Tricia Chilcott, "You've transformed our lives with this simple slice … It's AMAZING!"*

Makes 12

- *1 cup (230g) butter, softened*
- *⅔ cup (150g) sugar*
- *2¼ cups (400g) plain flour*
- *200g Toblerone, broken*

Preheat oven to 165°C. Using electric beaters, cream the butter and sugar until soft. Add the flour and gently mix until combined. Pat firmly into a paper-lined 20 x 30cm baking pan and bake for 20 minutes or until the top turns a light golden colour. Remove from oven and top immediately with the broken pieces of Toblerone, smattering evenly across the slice. Leave for 5 minutes, then using a spatula or flat spoon, spread the softened chocolate evenly over the slice. Refrigerate to cool and set for at least one hour. Using a hot knife, cut into scrumptious slices.

Parties

Best Ever Ice-cream Cake

Harrison Dines turned 10 last year and when his beautiful Mum, Melinda placed this cake in the centre of the table, his eyeballs nearly popped out of his head. It's a SUPERSTAR CAKE for any occasion!

Serves 12

- *2 litres chocolate mint ice-cream, slightly softened*
- *2 x 200g packets Chocolate Ripple biscuits*
- *2 punnets (500g) strawberries, hulled and halved*

Press half the ice-cream into a 20cm springform pan to form your first layer (about 2 to 3cm thick). Make sure you spread the ice-cream right to the outer edges. Top with a layer of roughly crushed biscuits. Place a layer of strawberries over the cookies, then press in the remainder of the ice-cream and sprinkle with the rest of the crushed cookies. Press a piece of baking paper or foil onto the top of the ice-cream cake. Freeze the cake overnight. The following day, release the sides of the springform pan and run a spatula or long, bladed knife around the edge of the cake. Place a serving plate on the top of the cake and quickly but gently turn the cake over. Remove the base and decorate with more strawberries and broken chocolate cookies. Once the cake is turned out of the pan, decorate quickly and serve immediately.

Optional: This awesome cake can be made with whatever flavour of ice-cream that takes your fancy; strawberry ripple, chocolate, vanilla or caramel crunch.

Bugs in Rugs

Makes 12

- *3 slices wholemeal bread, crusts removed*
- *½ cup (140g) tomato sauce*
- *¼ cup (60g) butter, melted*
- *12 cocktail frankfurters (Cheerios)*

Preheat oven 180°C. Pierce frankfurters all over with a fork. Using a rolling pin, roll out the slices of bread to flatten slightly. Spread tomato sauce on the bread, then cut into quarters. Place a frankfurter diagonally on each quarter of bread. Bring up edges and secure with a toothpick. Brush the bread liberally with the melted butter. Place on paper lined baking tray and bake for 10 minutes or until the bread is crisp and lightly browned. Serve warm.

Tip: Serve with a large jug of water but add a splash of colour to it by colouring ice-cubes with a couple of drops of food colouring.

Caramel Popcorn

SCRUM-DIDDILY-UMPTIOUS!

Serves 6

- *8 cups (320g) popped popcorn*
- *½ cup (160g) honey*
- *½ cup (130g) smooth peanut butter*
- *3 tablespoons (45g) butter*

Place the popcorn in a large bowl. In a small saucepan, boil the honey for 5 minutes. Stir in the peanut butter and butter. Pour over the popcorn and mix well to coat.

Optional: A tasty savoury option is to buy microwave buttery popcorn, pop it, pour into a large bowl and coat with grated parmesan cheese and a sprinkle of paprika.

Tip: Unpopped popcorn can be stored in an airtight container for about 1 year. I have read where it is best stored in the refrigerator or freezer because the kernels will retain more of their natural moisture and pop up larger and fluffier.

Chocolate Crackles

f *A quick, easy and truly delicious recipe from the beautiful Melanie Roberts.*

Makes 24

- *200g milk or dark chocolate, broken up*
- *½ cup (115g) butter, softened*
- *3 cups (240g) Coco Pops*

Line 24 mini muffin cups with paper liners. In a large saucepan, combine the chocolate and butter and melt over medium-low heat. Stir in the cereal, coating thoroughly. Divide among the muffin cups and refrigerate for 2 hours to set.

Optional: Coco Pops and Rice Bubbles are interchangeable, depending what you have in your cupboard … Gotta love that!

You Tube *4 Ingredients Channel / Chocolate Crackles*

Chocolate Fruit Jewels

I cannot tell you how many little girls I've impressed with this easy, elegant recipe … 4 Ingredients will be in your life for a looooong time with this little gem!

Serves 8

- *250g milk chocolate, broken up*
- *½ cup coloured 100s & 1000s (sprinkles)*
- *225g seedless grapes, washed and dried*

In a microwaveable bowl, melt the chocolate in 30-second increments, stirring after each, until smooth and creamy. Fill a small cup with sprinkles. Using a toothpick or a fork, dip each grape completely in chocolate, shake gently to remove excess chocolate then dip or roll in the sprinkles and place on a paper lined baking tray. When they are all done, pop them in the fridge to set the chocolate, about 20 minutes.

When you want something expensive,
ask your Grandparents!

Matthew, age 12

Heart Me Toasties

I got the idea for 'Toasties' on our Facebook page when one of our lovely American Moms was telling us that her kids love toasted sandwiches cut into shapes and served on kebab sticks …
Thanks Trudi – so do we ALL now!

Makes 12

- *6 slices wholemeal bread*
- *2 tablespoons butter*
- *½ cup grated cheddar cheese*
- *12 medium kebab sticks*

Lay each slice of bread onto a flat, clean surface and butter just one side. Using a heart cookie-cutter, cut four hearts from each slice. On the unbuttered side of 12 sprinkle with cheese then place the other 12 hearts, butter-side up, on top. Lightly toast in a sandwich press or in a non-stick frying pan over medium heat until nice and golden. Gently push a stick into the bottom of the heart. Serve immediately.

Tip: I placed an orange in the box in this picture and gently pressed the kebab sticks in it to hold firm.

Jelly Fish

These were the toast of my 3 year old's party last year, his little friends adored them.

Makes 8

- *2 packets (75g) jelly crystals, yellow and blue*
- *100g packet of 'fish' lollies*

Make up the yellow jelly as per the packet instructions and fill the base of 8 plastic cups evenly. Refrigerate for 30 minutes or until just setting, gently push a fish into the jelly (I used a kebab stick to push it beneath the surface. Refrigerate until set. Make up the blue packet of jelly crystals as per the packet instructions, and and pour the mixture evenly across the 8 cups. Refrigerate for 30 minutes or until just setting, then gently push another fish into the jelly. The jelly needs to be just setting otherwise your fishy will float to the top like it ain't feeling too well – if you know what I mean!!!! Refrigerate for at least 3 to 4 hours to completely set.

Amanda Smith gave us this easy suggestion calling it "Snake Pits". Make two packets of green jelly crystals as per the packet instructions, then pour into 6 plastic wine goblets. Leave to cool for 30 minutes before adding 2 snake lollies to each goblet, ensuring their heads hang out over the edge. Refrigerate for a few hours to set ... The kids love them!

Octopus Dip

This is my 10 year olds all-time FAVOURITE dip. It took me several months to get around to trying it but when I did I made up for lost time, it's simply sensational!

Serves 8

- *½ cup creamy mayonnaise (I used Praise)*
- *½ cup sour cream*
- *1 garlic clove, crushed*
- *1 red capsicum (pepper)*

In a bowl, mix the first three ingredients together, cover with cling film and sit in the fridge for 15 minutes. Meanwhile cut the top third from a capsicum (for the body of the octopus) and slice 8 long thin strips from the bottom two-thirds (for tentacles). When ready to serve, spoon the dip into a dish, pop the lid of the capsicum in the centre and surround with '8 legs.'

Optional: Give your octopus googly eyes - I used blueberries (held into place with tooth picks). You could also use sultanas or raisins or even whole cloves.

 I love this dip, it's PERFECT to serve with a mezze of fresh, raw veggie sticks and florets as dippers. In particular, carrot, celery, cauliflower and broccoli.

Partysicles

Packed with your kid's favourite fruits, each bite bursts with flavour and is a healthy, colourful addition to any birthday party.

Makes 8 ❄

- *100g strawberries, cut into approximately 1cm cubes*
- *¼ small rockmelon (cantaloupe), rind removed, cut into approximately 1cm cubes*
- *1 kiwifruit, peeled and cut into approximately 1cm cubes*
- *2 oranges, juiced*

In a bowl, combine the strawberries, rockmelon, and kiwifruit and mix thoroughly. Spoon into popsicle molds or plastic cups and divide the orange juice among them. Freeze for 4 to 5 hours or until frozen.

Optional: Pop any leftover fruit cubes into little plastic cocktail glasses and serve as 'Fruitilicious Cups'.

Peanut Butter & Chocolate Shards

This is almost too good for words, that glorious combination of chocolate and peanut butter is to die for!

Serves 8

- *200g white chocolate, coarsely chopped or broken*
- *1¾ cups (450g) smooth or crunchy peanut butter*
- *200g milk chocolate, coarsely chopped*

Line a 20 x 30cm baking tin with baking paper. Find two bowls, and in the first melt the white chocolate and peanut butter together in a microwave stirring every 30 seconds until nice and creamy. Pour the mixture into the baking tin and spread evenly. In the second bowl, repeat the process with milk chocolate, stirring every 30 seconds until smooth. Drizzle the melted milk chocolate over the peanut butter mixture. With a knife, cut through in swirls. Refrigerate until set and then cut into shards to serve.

Princess Pops

Makes 30

- *600g mudcake with icing*
- *400g white chocolate*
- *1 teaspoon vegetable oil*
- *½ cup pink sprinkles*

Into a large bowl break up the mudcake and mix until combined. Using wet hands, roll the mixture into balls 3cm in diameter, press gently on either side, molding the ball into a bell then place on a baking tray, pushing down gently to flatten the base. Continue until all the mixture is gone. Place the bells in the freezer for 1 hour. Just before removing, break the white chocolate up into a large dry bowl and microwave on high stirring every 30 seconds until the mixture is nice and smooth, stirring regularly. Then add the oil and stir well to thin the chocolate, this makes it easier to work with. Using a fork, dip each bell into the white chocolate. Drain off excess chocolate then sit in the pink sprinkles to cover the base and just up the sides to form the lining of the 'Princess's Gown!' With a small spatula lift back onto the tray then into the top of the 'bell' gently press in the Princess Pop until she sits neatly on the crest. Repeat for all.

I bought my Princess Pops online from www.wilton.com, or get your little princess busy designing, drawing and cutting our her own pretty princess faces and tape them to pop sticks. This is also a great little girls party activity!

Rainbow Rolls

Makes 4

- *4 slices of pastrami*
- *1 cup leftover cooked rice*
- *½ avocado*
- *1 carrot peeled*

Onto a clean surface place the slices of pastrami. Along the middle of each place the rice. Using a knife, cut thin slices of carrot and avocado and lay them on top of the rice. Roll the pastrami up, and secure with a toothpick. Serve as is or sliced in half.

 Use any number of the following fillings; corn, cucumber ribbons, thinly sliced red capsicum (pepper), sliced omelette, hummus, green beans, sliced snow peas, toasted almonds and mashed sweet potato.

Scrolls

 I love scrolls, they are a way to smuggle all kinds of glorious veggies into the growing bodies of kids ... Simply chop and scatter!

Makes 24

- *2 square sheets puff pastry, halved*
- *¼ cup tomato paste or spaghetti sauce*
- *100g ham, chopped*
- *1 cup grated cheddar cheese*

Preheat oven to 200°C. Line 3 baking trays with baking paper. Place pastry, 1 sheet at a time, onto a clean chopping board. Spread the tomato paste over each and sprinkle with ham and cheese. Starting from the edge nearest you, roll up the pastry. Cut each roll into quarters, then cut each quarter in three. Place the scrolls, cut-side up, onto the baking trays 2cm apart. Bake for 15 to 20 minutes or until the pastry is golden and the cheese melted. Allow to cool slightly before serving.

Optional: Brush the pastry scroll tops with beaten egg for a rich, golden finish.

Soda-Pop Cupcakes

f Submitted by Mel Roberts and are truly one of the EASIEST Cupcakes I have ever made.

Makes 12 ❄

- *340g packet vanilla cake-mix*
- *1 cup (250ml) soda-pop (I used creaming soda)*

Preheat oven to 180°C. Into a large bowl, pour the cake mix. Then add the soda. Stir together with a wooden spoon until combined. Line a 12-hole cupcake tin with papers and spoon the mixture evenly among each. Bake for 15 minutes or until puffy and cooked through.

Tip: In this recipe, you are substituting soda (soft drink) for the eggs, water, and oil or butter. The cupcakes will taste slightly like the soda you used and the combinations you can use are endless ... Enjoy the experiment and the EASE!

You Tube *4 Ingredients Channel / Soda Pop Cupcakes*

Strawberry Garden

Makes 24

- *500g strawberries, with stems if possible*
- *200g dark or milk chocolate, broken*
- *½ cup 100s & 1000s or coloured sprinkles*
- *24 kebab sticks*

Wash and dry the strawberries (leaving the stems in place). Gently push a stick into the base of each. Place the dark chocolate in a microwaveable bowl. Melt chocolate in 30-second increments, stirring after each, until smooth and creamy. Dip each strawberry into the chocolate, rotating it slowly. Lift it out and allow the excess to drain back into the bowl. Stand the stick in a tall glass or vase. Let cool slightly before dipping into the sprinkles. Repeat the process until all strawberries are coated. Refrigerate for 20 minutes to set the chocolate.

Optional: For the photograph, I placed an orange in the bucket and stood the the sticks in it.

Tip: Strawberries are the only fruit with seeds on the outside. Each berry has about 200 seeds. When choosing strawberries, always look for the ones red in colour to the hull. A full colouration usually means a naturally sweeter flavour.

Sweet Sesame Sausages

Makes 12

- *12 chipolatas*
- *2 tablespoons honey*
- *2 tablespoons sesame seeds*
- *12 medium kebab sticks*

Preheat the oven to 180°C. Line a baking tray with baking paper. Arrange the chipolatas on the tray and bake for 15 minutes. Drain off any fat. Drizzle with the honey and bake, turning a couple of times, until the sausages are sticky and golden all over, about 10 minutes. Sprinkle with the sesame seeds and bake for a final 5 minutes. Remove, cool and serve on a kebab stick to stave off those sticky fingers!

Optional: Mini-Meatballs, take 6 sausages, cut one end of the case from each sausage and squeeze a bite-size amount onto a baking tray. Each sausage should yield around 8 meatballs. Bake in a 180°C oven for 10 minutes or until cooked. Serve with a little tomato sauce to dip and watch them flyyyy!

You**Tube** *4 Ingredients Channel / Sweet Sesame Sausages*

Party Bag Ideas

It's AMAZING how quickly the cost of filling a party bag escalates when you are buying several 'little' items. Here are a few ideas we thought really clever for a lasting memory.

4 Ingredients

OKAAAAY so we are biased, but buy them on sale and have the birthday child sign each on his favourite recipe.

Animals

Buy some cheap animals eg., turtles, dinosaurs, farm animals at your local discount store and pop a lovely little 'Thank you' note around their necks.

Books

For each guest, hand-pick a small paperback or Little Golden Book to suit him or her.

Bubbles

Kids loooove bubbles!

Crayons and small pads

It may be just what is required to unleash your child's inner Picasso.

Disposable Camera

Expect to pay as little as $7 for a 24-exposure disposable camera.

Fake Tattoos

Come on Mum … You know you want one too!

Flashlight & batteries

Something a household never seems to have enough of!

Picture Frame

Take a photo of each child with the birthday boy or girl, print it and pop it in the frame to take home.

Piggy Bank

Give every child a piggy bank and pop their first $1 coin into it.

Plant Seeds

A 'budding' gardener may enjoy a packet of tomato seeds or their first mint plant (very hard to kill, it's a goodie to start with!)

Playdough

A little tub of playdough is fun for everyone.

Tape measure

What little boy doesn't like a tape measure?

Tiaras

Shop around for costume jewellery, as there are plenty of bargains for future princesses.

Water pistols

Fun for both boys and girls.

Great Party Games

Gods & Goddesses

4+ players

This game requires fairly mellow music. Give each child a book. When the music starts, the children walk around the room balancing the books on their heads. When the music stops, the children must try to go down on one knee. If their book falls off, he or she is eliminated. The music starts again and the game continues. The last child left in the game is the winner.

I went to Mars ...

6+ players

The children sit in a circle. The birthday child announces *"I went to Mars and I took a…"* then names any object e.g. my soccer ball. The next child has to repeat this and add another e.g. I went to Mars and I took a soccer ball and an apple," The third child will add a new object, always keeping the list in order. The game continues around the circle for as long as possible.

Jump the Broom

4+ players

Pop a broom on the ground. Play music as the children skip around in a circle, jumping over the broom. When the music stops, the child jumping over the broom, or the last child to jump the broom, is out. Continue until there is one child left.

Lolly Relay

6+ players

Divide the children into two teams and have them form lines. Give the first child in each line a pair of mittens. Give everyone a wrapped lolly. When you say "go", the first player in each line puts on the mittens, unwraps the candy and pops it into their mouth. Then, they quickly take the mittens off and hand them to the second person in line. The second player does the same, and so on down the line. The team that finishes first wins.

Optional: For a healthier twist, use chocolate dipped strawberries, or apple quarters.
Eventually children will flinch or move and you will get a winner.

Memory on a Tray

4+ players

Place a number of objects on a tray in no particular order while the children are in another room or focusing on a different activity. A variety of shapes and sizes work best. For example, a paper clip, fifty cent piece, balloon, biscuit, envelope, fork, etc. The number of objects included is best dictated by the age of the participants — place more objects for older groups and fewer for younger groups. When the children are ready, set the tray down for less than 60 seconds (again, this is best dictated by the children's ages) and then remove it from the room. The children then write down each of the objects they remember from the tray. Whoever is able to list the most objects accurately wins! It's always fun to bring the tray back in and remind the group what was there.

Please let us know on facebook.com/4ingredientspage which of these games you played and liked the best!

Index

Invitation

Join our Foodie Family

At 4 Ingredients we cultivate a family of busy people all bound together by the desire to create good, healthy, homemade meals quickly, easily and economically.

Our aim is to save us all precious time and money in the kitchen.
If this is you too, then we invite you to join our growing family where we share kitchen wisdom daily.

If you have a favourite recipe, or a tip that has worked for you in your kitchen and think others would enjoy it, please join our family at:

f facebook.com/4ingredientspage

P @4ingredients

You Tube 4 Ingredients Channel

www 4ingredients.com.au

y @4ingredients

With Love
Kim